ST.
PATRICK'S DAY
Alphabet

ST. PATRICK'S DAY
Alphabet

Beverly Barras Vidrine

Illustrated by Patrick Soper

PELICAN PUBLISHING COMPANY
Gretna 2002

First printing, January 2001
Second printing, January 2002
Third printing, January 2002

For my husband, Dennis

Library of Congress Cataloging-in-Publication Data

Vidrine, Beverly Barras.
St. Patrick's day alphabet / Beverly Barras Vidrine ; illustrated by Patrick Soper.
p. cm.
Summary: For each letter of the alphabet, presents and defines a word relating to Saint
Patrick or the holiday that celebrates him.
ISBN: 1-56554-719-5 (pbk.)
1. Saint Patrick's Day—Juvenile literature. 2. English language—Alphabet—Juvenile
literature. [1. Saint Patrick's Day. 2. Holidays. 3. Alphabet.] I. Title: Saint Patrick's day
alphabet. II. Soper, Patrick, ill. III. Title.

GT4995.P3 V53 2000
394.262—dc21
[[E]]

99-087583

Published by Pelican Publishing Company, Inc.
1000 Burmaster Street, Gretna, Louisiana 70053

ST. PATRICK'S DAY
Alphabet

About four hundred years after Jesus was born, a man named Patrick went to Ireland. Patrick had a mission. He wanted to tell the Irish people about Jesus. So Patrick and his helpers traveled almost all over Ireland. Patrick baptized most of the Irish people. He taught many Irish to read and write.

The Irish people had much respect for Patrick. After he died, they prayed to him, and he became their patron saint. Then they chose a day to remember him. St. Patrick's Day is a celebration of Irish ways.

A is for accordion, the Irish squeezebox used to play dance music on St. Patrick's Day. Many accordion players listen to Irish music to learn the rhythm of the old Irish tunes.

B is for bodhran (BOW-rawn), the flat, one-sided Irish drum. It is the most popular drum played in Irish folk music, especially around this holiday.

C is for céilí (KAY-lee), an Irish dance party. In the old days, Irish people gathered at crossroads for a céilí. Now people do Irish dances in towns on this day and all year long.

D is for Druid (DROO-id), a member of a religion in Ireland a very long time ago. Patrick told many Druids about Christ, and some became Christians.

E is for "Everybody is Irish," a favorite saying on St. Patrick's Day. Almost everybody, Irish or not, celebrates on that day.

F is for folktale, a story passed on from one person to another. One old Irish folktale says Patrick drove all the snakes out of Ireland.

G is for green, like the grass covering the hills of Ireland. The color gives this island its nickname, the Emerald Isle. On this Irish holiday, the color green is seen almost everywhere.

H is for harp, a national emblem of Ireland. Long ago, Irishmen told stories while this musical instrument was played. Today, many St. Patrick's Day celebrations feature harp music.

is for Irish, the people of Ireland. They love St. Patrick and their music, songs, and dance. Those who move away still keep these traditions.

J is for jig, an Irish stepdance. Irish dancers' feet move fast, up and down, back and forth. Even their parents and grandparents danced the jig on St. Patrick's Day.

K is for Kells, a town in Ireland where Patrick's followers built a monastery. The monks there made the Book of Kells. It has designs and tiny pictures explaining the gospel.

L is for leprechaun, a fairy in old Irish tales. A story says that anyone catching this shoemaker might find a pot of gold. In time, the playful sprite became a symbol of St. Patrick's Day.

M is for March 17, the day the Irish honor St. Patrick by going to church. Afterward, they celebrate with parades and Irish music.

N is for New York City, which holds a big St. Patrick's Day parade. Irish groups and marching bands walk up Fifth Avenue in front of St. Patrick's Cathedral.

O is for oak, a tree well known for its wood. Long ago in Ireland, a stick cut from an oak tree was called a shillelagh (shuh-LAY-lee). Later, walking sticks made of wood had that Irish name. Sometimes people carry shillelaghs in St. Patrick's Day parades.

P is for Patrick, the famous bishop of Ireland, who preached the gospel to the Irish. By living a holy life he became known as St. Patrick.

Q is for Quoilé (kwul), a river in Northern Ireland. After Patrick died, he was buried nearby. The town of Downpatrick, named for him, is located close to this river.

R is for religion, to serve and adore God. When Patrick was a boy, he said about a hundred prayers a day. Later, he studied religion for many years, and then he became a priest.

S is for shamrock, a three-leaf plant from Ireland. A legend says Patrick used this plant to explain the Holy Trinity—the Father, the Son, and the Holy Spirit.

T is for tricolor, a flag having three colors. The national flag of Ireland is a tricolor of green, white, and orange. The green stands for old Ireland, the white for peace, and the orange for new Ireland.

U is for uilleann (ILL-un), meaning elbow in Irish. It is the name of the bagpipes from Ireland that are played sitting down. Other bagpipes are played standing up. Uilleann pipers celebrate the holiday by playing folk and dance music.

V is for violin, also known as the fiddle. A fiddler makes a tune by moving the bow across the strings. Fiddles are popular at parties on St. Patrick's Day.

W is for "wee people," the tiny fairies in Irish folktales. Although some fairies like to sing and dance together, the leprechaun is always alone. The leprechaun is the only fairy associated with St. Patrick's Day.

X is for xylophone, a musical instrument played by striking hammers on bars. The xylophone is heard in some new Irish music. It is similar to the bell lyra played in marching bands for St. Patrick's Day parades.

Y is for Yeats (yates), an Irish poet whose full name is William Butler Yeats. His first great poem tells about St. Patrick.

Z is for zeal, a desire to do something, as when Patrick prayed. His love for God brought him to establish the Christian faith in Ireland.